DC COMICS™

BATSUITS AND CAPES
THE SCIENCE BEHIND BATMAN'S BODY ARMOR

BY AGNIESZKA BISKUP

BATMAN CREATED BY
BOB KANE

BATMAN™
SCIENCE

CAPSTONE PRESS
a capstone imprint

Published by Capstone Press in 2014

A Capstone Imprint

1710 Roe Crest Drive

North Mankato, Minnesota 56003

www.capstonepub.com

STAR30198

Library of Congress Cataloging-in-Publication Data

Biskup, Agnieszka.

 Batsuits and capes : the science behind Batman's body armor / by Agnieszka Biskup ; Batman created by Bob Kane.

     pages cm.—(Batman science)

 Includes bibliographical references and index.

 ISBN 978-1-4765-3942-3 (library binding)

 ISBN 978-1-4765-5210-1 (paperback)

 1. Batman (Fictitious character)—Juvenile literature. 2. Body armor—Juvenile literature. I. Kane, Bob. II. Title.

 PN6728.B36B64 2014

 741.5'3—dc23   2013028326

Summary: Explores the real-world science and engineering connections to the features of Batman's Batsuit.

Editorial Credits

Editor: Christopher L. Harbo

Designer: Veronica Scott

Production Specialist: Kathy McColley

Photo Credits

DoD photo by Staff Sgt. Stephen Schester, USAF, 11; Getty Images: Denver Post/Ernie Leyba, 21 (bottom); Glow Images: Science Faction/SuperStock, 14 (left); Newscom: ZUMA Press/ChinaFotoPress, 28, ZUMA Press/Daily Mail/David Crump, 29; Science Source: GIPhotoStock, 22; Shutterstock: 501room, 12 (right), Alexandra Lande, 27, ArtTomCat, 19, Carolina K. Smith MD, 14 (right), Distrikt 3, 16, Fotokostic, 12 (left), Mi.Ti., 10; U.S. Air Force photo by Senior Airman Felicia Juenke, 15, Staff Sgt. Stacy L. Pearsall, 6; U.S. Army photo by Kaye Richey, 7 (top), Melvin G. Tarpley, 7 (bottom); U.S. Navy Photo by Lt. Troy Wilcox, 24, MC2 Michael Lindsey, 17, MC2 Tony D. Curtis, 23, MC3 Billy Ho, 25, MCSN Jonathan L. Correa, 9; Wikimedia: J. Glover, Atlanta, Georgia, 21 (top)

Design Elements:Shutterstock: BiterBig, ClickHere, Jason Winter

 Printed in the United States of America in Stevens Point, Wisconsin.

 042015   008921R

TABLE OF CONTENTS

SUPER HERO SCIENCE AND ENGINEERING

Super heroes have battled crime in comic books and on the big screen for decades. While many of these heroes have amazing strength and incredible powers, Batman is a little different. He's not an alien from another planet. He doesn't wear magic rings or see through walls with X-ray vision. Under his suit and cape, the Dark Knight is a regular human being. He's Bruce Wayne of Gotham City.

But what Bruce lacks in superpowers, he easily makes up for with brains and brawn. As Batman, he relies on science and engineering to gain an advantage over his enemies. He uses the most state-of-the-art gear around—and his crime-fighting suit is no exception.

Originally, the Batsuit was just a disguise. While it made Batman look menacing, it had no special high-tech features. But as technology has changed, so has the Batsuit—and many of its features are rooted in reality. Need evidence? Get ready to check out the real-life science behind the Dark Knight's Batsuit.

FACT:

BATMAN MADE HIS FIRST APPEARANCE IN
DETECTIVE COMICS #27 IN 1939.

CHAPTER 1

BATSUIT BASICS

To fight crime on the mean streets of Gotham City, you need body armor. For Batman, the layers and pieces of his Batsuit are the key to staying safe. His skintight suit may look thin, but it offers more protection than meets the eye.

HIDING IN THE SHADOWS

As Batman keeps an eye on Gotham City's criminals, he doesn't want to be seen himself. It's no accident that his Batsuit uses mostly black and blue colors. The dark colors help him blend into the shadows.

In the real world, people use camouflage to avoid being seen. Camouflage, or camo, is coloring or covering that makes people, animals, or objects look like their surroundings. Soldiers wear different types of camo depending on where they are working. Most camo uses colors and patterns to hide something or someone.

A soldier wears green and gray camo to blend into her surroundings.

While camo can be a single color, patterns of different colored patches work best. This **mottled** pattern is called disruptive coloration. A soldier wearing green patterned camo in a jungle gives the brain a puzzle. Instead of seeing a soldier, the brain wants to connect the pattern's lines with the lines of the trees, leaves, and shadows. In this way, disruptive coloration helps disguise the shape of a person's body. A person wearing this type of camo appears to blend in with the surroundings.

Soldier uniforms use a variety of mottled patterns to match different surroundings.

PICKING COLORS

When it comes to color, camo is all about matching the environment. To hide in forests, soldiers wear green and brown to match the leaves, ground, and tree bark. For snowy areas, their camo uses a mixture of white and gray. The camo soldiers wear in deserts is sometimes called chocolate-chip camouflage. Its mixture of brown and tan looks similar to chocolate-chip cookies.

INTO THE FIRE

Batman's enemies know how to turn up the heat on the Caped Crusader. Luckily the materials in the Batsuit can survive fires and fiery explosions. Do these kinds of materials exist in the real world?

Ever since people started using fire, they've looked for ways to avoid being burned. For centuries, natural materials such as wool offered some fire protection. But more recently scientists started making breakthroughs. In the 1960s they created a heat and flame-resistant material called Nomex.

Nomex is made of ringlike **molecules** bonded together into tough, long chains. These chains create really strong fibers. Although Nomex burns when you hold it to a flame, it stops burning as soon as the flame is removed.

Just as important, Nomex fibers are poor **conductors** of heat. When fire touches Nomex, the woven fibers thicken and swell. This swelling creates a protective barrier between the heat source and the skin. The thickened fibers also prevent the material from melting or igniting. And it takes time for heat to travel through Nomex. Hopefully in those extra seconds, you've managed to put the fire out!

Firefighters on a U.S. Navy ship wear Nomex hoods to protect their heads and faces from fire.

FACT:

YOU MAY NOT REALIZE IT, BUT YOU PROBABLY HAVE NOMEX IN YOUR HOUSE. IT'S USED IN MANY OVEN GLOVES.

molecule—the atoms making up the smallest unit of a substance

conductor—a material that lets heat, electricity, or sound travel easily through it

BODY ARMOR

To fight crime, Batman puts himself in the line of fire. The Batsuit is the only thing that stands between him and all kinds of lethal impacts. To protect him, it includes body armor—a technology that has come a long way over the centuries.

The history of body armor spans thousands of years. Ancient tribes used animal hides and woven plant material for protection from cuts and scrapes. The ancient Romans covered their chests with metal breastplates. Full-body metal armor came into its glory by the 1400s. Medieval knights covered themselves from head to toe in metal plates to protect against sword thrusts or arrows.

Once cannons and guns were developed, traditional armor fell by the wayside. To protect from these kinds of impacts, metal armor would be too thick and heavy to wear.

Medieval knights protected themselves with heavy metal armor.

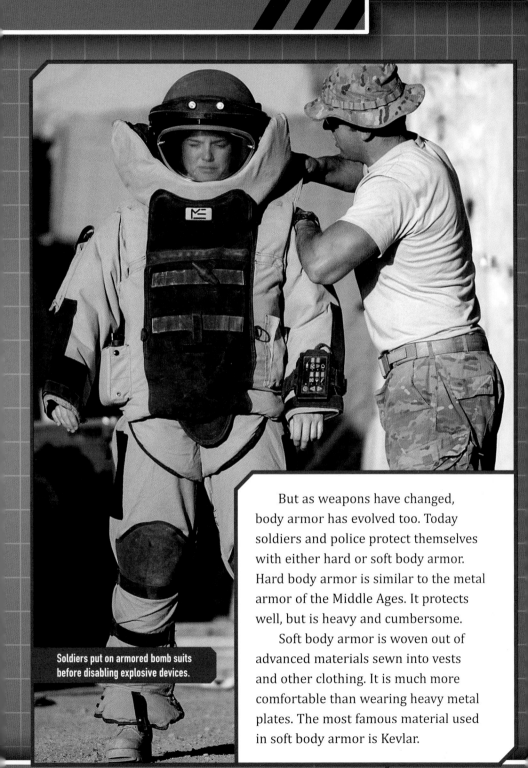

Soldiers put on armored bomb suits before disabling explosive devices.

But as weapons have changed, body armor has evolved too. Today soldiers and police protect themselves with either hard or soft body armor. Hard body armor is similar to the metal armor of the Middle Ages. It protects well, but is heavy and cumbersome.

Soft body armor is woven out of advanced materials sewn into vests and other clothing. It is much more comfortable than wearing heavy metal plates. The most famous material used in soft body armor is Kevlar.

KEVLAR

Like Nomex, Kevlar is another amazing **synthetic** material found in the real world. Lightweight and flexible, Kevlar is about five times stronger than steel. Its stretching strength is eight times greater than steel wire.

Kevlar is strong due to its chemical structure. Its long molecule chains are naturally arranged in regular **parallel** lines, like spaghetti in a package. But the chains also form bonds between each other, as if you've glued all the spaghetti together. This makes the material extraordinarily tough.

Inside police vests are many layers of tightly woven Kevlar.

synthetic—something that is made by people rather than found in nature
parallel—to be in a straight line and an equal distance apart

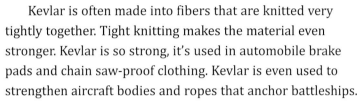

Kevlar is often made into fibers that are knitted very tightly together. Tight knitting makes the material even stronger. Kevlar is so strong, it's used in automobile brake pads and chain saw-proof clothing. Kevlar is even used to strengthen aircraft bodies and ropes that anchor battleships.

Kevlar can be woven and used to protect any part of the body. In fact, Nomex and Kevlar can be blended together to protect against fire, cuts, and impacts. Firefighter gear is often made of a Nomex and Kevlar mix. But the most well-known use of Kevlar is in bulletproof vests.

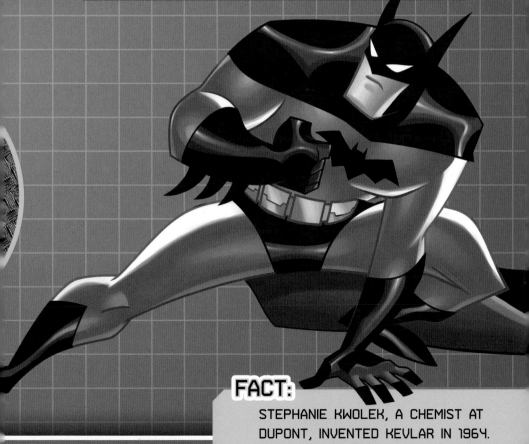

FACT:

STEPHANIE KWOLEK, A CHEMIST AT DUPONT, INVENTED KEVLAR IN 1964.

CERAMIC PLATES

Sometimes soldiers or police need more than Kevlar protection. For that they turn to hard body armor. This armor is often made of steel or **ceramic** plates.

STRIKE FACE

ceramic plate

Steel is very durable and less expensive, but it is heavy to wear. Ceramic plates are used to make light armor that offers excellent protection. These plates are as strong as steel but 70 percent lighter. Ceramic plates can be made of various materials. Some of the strongest are made of a powder called boron carbide. This powder is pressed and heated to about 4,000 degrees Fahrenheit (2,204 degrees Celsius). After baking, the plates are nearly as hard as diamond.

Ceramic plates will still shatter on impact, but that's not a bad thing. Shattering the plate spreads out and reduces the energy of a bullet or blow.

ceramic—having to do with objects made out of clay

A DIFFICULT CHOICE

In real life, soldiers and police have to compromise between safety and mobility. To move easily, they can wear less or lighter armor. But that means their level of protection decreases. If they wear heavier armor with more protection, they weigh themselves down. Heavier armor makes it harder for officers to move or respond quickly. For police and soldiers in the line of fire, it's a difficult choice to make.

A soldier puts on a body armor vest before a mission in Afghanistan.

Brawling with archenemies can be tough on any crime fighter's hands and feet. That's why gloves and boots are key parts of Batman's suit. But these common pieces of clothing hide more science than meets the eye.

GLOVES AND GAUNTLETS

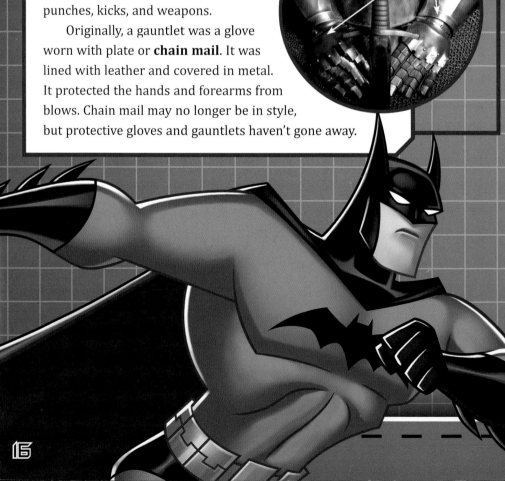

gauntlets

The long gloves Batman wears are called **gauntlets**. They give his hands and arms much needed protection from punches, kicks, and weapons.

Originally, a gauntlet was a glove worn with plate or **chain mail**. It was lined with leather and covered in metal. It protected the hands and forearms from blows. Chain mail may no longer be in style, but protective gloves and gauntlets haven't gone away.

All sorts of people from lumberjacks to chefs use gloves and gauntlets. They protect workers from assembly-line blades, knives, sheet metal, and chain saws. Chemists use gauntlets to protect their forearms and hands from dangerous chemical spills. Shoulder-length Kevlar gauntlets help protect the arms of soldiers from flying metal and other dangers.

Many athletes also wear protective gauntlets as part of their uniforms. Kendo and fencing both require gloves and gauntlets. In kendo, long thickly padded fabric and leather gloves called *kote* protect the forearms, wrists, and hands. Fencers wear lightly padded gloves that may be made of leather or of washable materials.

Welders wear thick gauntlets to protect their hands from burns.

gauntlet—a long protective glove

chain mail—armor made up of thousands of tiny iron rings linked together

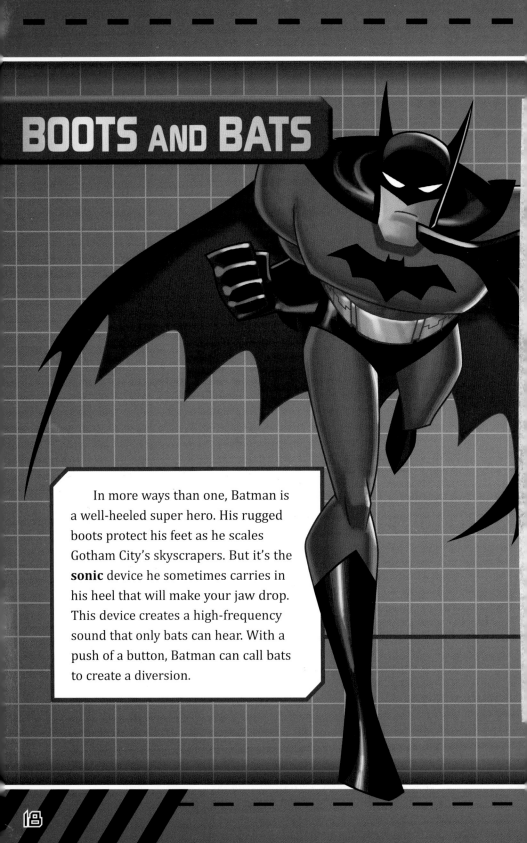

BOOTS AND BATS

In more ways than one, Batman is a well-heeled super hero. His rugged boots protect his feet as he scales Gotham City's skyscrapers. But it's the **sonic** device he sometimes carries in his heel that will make your jaw drop. This device creates a high-frequency sound that only bats can hear. With a push of a button, Batman can call bats to create a diversion.

Real-world scientists don't have sonic devices to call bats. But they do use loudspeakers, microphones, and special electronic "ears" to study the sounds bats make. Bats send out high-frequency sound waves that bounce off objects in their paths. People can't hear these sounds, but bats can. They listen to the echoes of these sounds to locate nearby objects. Their incredible power is known as **echolocation**.

Insect-eating bats use echolocation to find food. They keep track of the time between making a sound and hearing its echo return. A bat's echolocation system is very precise. Scientists study it in hopes of making radar and sonar equipment even better.

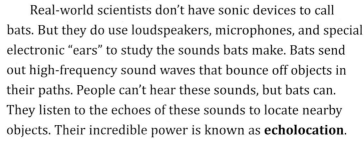

FACT:

IN 1940 SCIENTIST DONALD GRIFFIN DISCOVERED BATS USE SOUND TO FIND THEIR WAY IN THE DARK. HE COINED THE WORD "ECHOLOCATION" TO DESCRIBE WHAT THEY DO.

sonic—having to do with sound waves
echolocation—the process of using sounds and echoes to locate objects

CHAPTER 3

COWL CONSTRUCTION

To hide his identity, Batman wears a cowl. This hooded mask disguises his features and makes him look threatening. But the cowl does a lot more than look cool. It protects his head from impacts. It also has a bunch of amazing devices built in.

LONG-DISTANCE HEARING

One key to fighting crime is to figure out what criminals are up to. To do this, the "ears" of Batman's cowl carry microphones. These microphones send audio to a sound **amplifier**. Batman can hear anything he's pointed at, even if he's not near the target.

In the real world, long-distance eavesdropping is done with parabolic microphones. These listening devices use a bowl-shaped reflector to collect and focus sound waves onto a receiver. They collect sound waves the same way a satellite dish collects radio waves. Such microphones pick up sounds from 300 yards (274 meters) away. People use parabolic microphones to record sounds from nature and to collect audio from football sidelines. They are also used in police **surveillance** and for spying.

A parabolic microphone picks up the sounds of the game from the sidelines.

People can also listen in on conversations using tiny devices called bugs. Bugs are hidden microphones that secretly pick up sounds and send them to transmitters or receivers. Bugs can be disguised as batteries or appliance plugs. They can be as small as pencil erasers, making them easy to hide in walls or furniture.

Bugs use miniature microphones that are smaller than a fingertip.

amplifier—a piece of equipment that makes sound louder

surveillance—the act of keeping very close watch on someone, someplace, or something

SEEING IN THE DARK

Just like a bat, Batman is most active at night. But even the Dark Knight needs help peering through the gloom. To boost his eyesight, Batman's cowl often includes night-vision lenses. These high-tech specs help him see in the dark.

Seeing in the dark starts with the science of light. Light energy travels in waves of different lengths. The light we can see is called visible light. But some light waves are too short or too long for us to see. The shorter waves include gamma rays, X-rays, and ultraviolet rays. The longer waves include infrared light, microwaves, and radio waves.

Thermal imaging shows hot water running from a faucet.

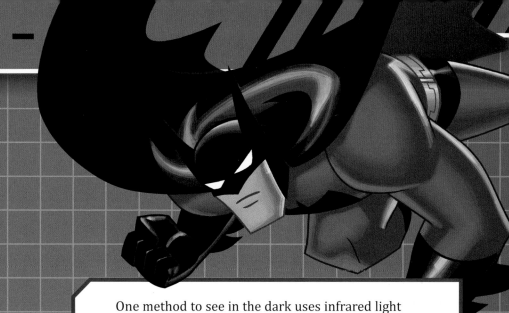

One method to see in the dark uses infrared light instead of visible light. Infrared light waves carry heat. All objects give off infrared light waves. Thermal imaging picks up these waves and changes them into visible light. Thermal night-vision goggles let you see people, animals, and objects by the heat patterns they give off. They don't need any visible light at all.

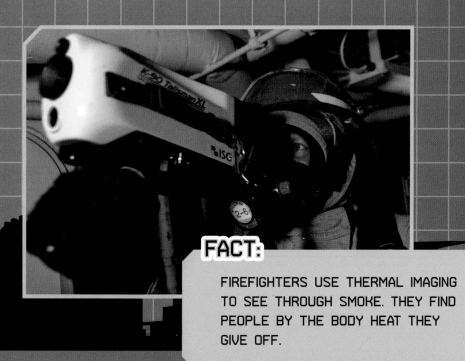

FACT:

FIREFIGHTERS USE THERMAL IMAGING TO SEE THROUGH SMOKE. THEY FIND PEOPLE BY THE BODY HEAT THEY GIVE OFF.

ENHANCING THE IMAGE

Thermal imaging isn't the only way people see in the dark. Most night-vision gear uses image enhancement. This technology creates the eerie, glowing green night-vision images people see in movies.

Image enhancement collects any available light and makes the most of it. Even in the dimmest conditions, all objects reflect some light. Night-vision goggles with image enhancement use an image-intensifier tube. It gathers and boosts available light to make objects look brighter. Unfortunately, some of the detail and all of the color is lost during the enhancement process.

So why do objects seen with image enhancement look green instead of black and white? Night-vision goggles produce green pictures because human eyes are most sensitive to green light. The human eye can make out more shades of green than any other color.

THERMAL OR ENHANCED?

Which night-vision technology is better? That depends on what you're looking for. Thermal imaging can be used day or night in smoke, fog, and dust storms. But the equipment is more expensive, larger, and heavier. Image enhancement only works in the dark, but it is cheaper and the images are also easier to make out. But camouflage can still trick image enhancement technology. Thermal imaging, however, can find hidden objects by the heat they give off.

A soldier tests the settings on a night-vision scope.

We've all seen Batman perched atop one of Gotham City's skyscrapers. His watchful eye scans the city. His cape flaps in the wind. But Batman's cape doesn't only make him look like an awesome super hero. It also helps him glide safely through the air.

GLIDING THROUGH GOTHAM CITY

Batman's ability to glide is similar to how hang gliders work. A hang glider is basically a curved triangle-shaped wing. The wing lets air flow over its surface to make it rise. Hang glider pilots rise into the air by taking off from mountaintops, cliffs, or other high spots. The movement of air over the surface of the wing generates lift, the force that counters **gravity**. This force keeps the glider aloft.

gravity—a force that pulls objects with mass together; gravity pulls objects down toward the center of Earth

Powered aircraft require a motor, propeller, or jet engines to stay up in the air. Hang gliders need air movement. If the air is still, the glider will fall at a rate of roughly 200 feet (61 m) per minute. To stay aloft, a glider pilot needs to find and use thermals. These columns of warm air occur when the sun heats the air and causes it to rise. A pilot catches a thermal by circling the warm air, which pushes him or her upward. Strong thermals can lift a hang glider thousands of feet in minutes!

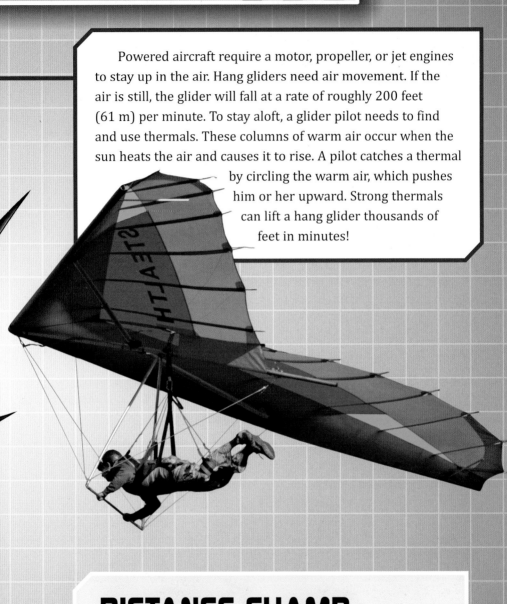

DISTANCE CHAMP

Hang glider pilots can easily fly 100 miles (161 kilometers) in a single flight. But Dustin Martin did better than that. In 2012 he set the world record for distance by traveling 474 miles (763 km) from Zapata to Lorenzo, Texas. The flight took just more than 11 hours.

WINGSUIT FLYING

Batman's cape makes gliding to the ground look easy. In real life, gliding is a little trickier—and more dangerous. But it's not impossible. Some thrill seekers wear wingsuits to jump from extreme heights and glide through the air.

Wingsuits have webbed wing surfaces between the legs and under the arms. During a jump, the air inflates these surfaces by passing through inlets in the suit. The suit becomes a giant wing. It makes the wingsuiter look like a huge flying squirrel.

Wingsuiters deal with the same forces of flight that planes and hang gliders do. When a wingsuiter jumps out of a plane, gravity pulls him or her down. The average skydiver falls to Earth at a rate of 120 miles (193 km) per hour. Wingsuits cut that speed by more than half. Wingsuiters can land safely because they use parachutes to slow themselves down before reaching the ground.

A wingsuiter glides through the air above Tianmen Mountain in China.

GARY CONNERY

In 2012 a British daredevil named Gary Connery completed a 2,400-foot (732-m) wingsuit dive from a helicopter. He dived into an area stacked with nearly 19,000 cardboard boxes to help cushion his fall. Connery became the first person in the world to jump out of an aircraft and land safely without using a parachute.

BATSUIT EVOLUTION

Batman's suit started as a simple disguise, but it evolved into a technological marvel. From fire resistance to bullet deflection, the Batsuit is the ultimate super hero body armor. Best of all, it reflects the science and engineering all around us. What kind of features will the Caped Crusader's suit have in the years to come? No one knows for sure. But keep an eye on real-world advancements in science and technology. They'll likely show up in the Batsuit.

GLOSSARY

amplifier (AM-pluh-fy-uhr)—a piece of equipment that makes sound louder

ceramic (suh-RA-mik)—having to do with objects made out of clay

chain mail (CHAYN MAYL)—armor made up of thousands of tiny iron rings linked together

conductor (kuhn-DUHK-tuhr)—a material that lets heat, electricity, or sound travel easily through it

echolocation (eh-koh-loh-KAY-shuhn)—the process of using sounds and echoes to locate objects; bats use echolocation to find food

gauntlet (GAWNT-lit)—a long protective glove

gravity (GRAV-uh-tee)—a force that pulls objects with mass together; gravity pulls objects down toward the center of Earth

molecule (MOL-uh-kyool)—the atoms making up the smallest unit of a substance; H_2O is a molecule of water

mottled (MOT-uhld)—covered in patches of different colors

parallel (PA-ruh-lel)—to be in a straight line and an equal distance apart

sonic (SON-ik)—having to do with sound waves

surveillance (suhr-VAY-luhnss)—the act of keeping very close watch on someone, someplace, or something

synthetic (sin-THET-ik)—something that is made by people rather than found in nature